The Rockwool Foundation Research Unit

Study Paper No. 20

Immigrant and Native Children's Cognitive Outcomes and the Effect of Ethnic Concentration in Danish Schools

Peter Jensen and
Astrid Würtz Rasmussen

University Press of Southern Denmark

Odense 2008

Immigrant and Native Children's Cognitive Outcomes and the Effect of Ethnic Concentration in Danish Schools

Study Paper No. 20

Published by:

Address:
The Rockwool Foundation Research Unit
Sejroegade 11
DK-2100 Copenhagen

Telephone	+45 39 17 38 32
Fax	+45 39 20 52 19
E-mail	forskningsenheden@rff.dk
Home page	www.rff.dk

ISBN 978-87-90199-13-5
ISSN 0908-3979
November 2008
Print run: 300
Printed by Special-Trykkeriet Viborg a-s

Price: 90,00 DKK, including 25% VAT

Foreword

In 2004 the Rockwool Foundation decided to launch a research project that would focus upon the relationship of young immigrants to the Danish educational system, including an investigation of the attitudes of these young people towards education and of the benefits that they obtained from attending primary and lower secondary school (i.e. the obligatory stages of schooling) in Denmark. It has been evident for a number of years that non-Western immigrants do not make much use of the Danish educational system, and that far too many of those who do go to Danish educational institutions fail to complete their courses. If this educational pattern of non-achievement is not broken, then it will greatly hinder the true integration of immigrants from non-Western backgrounds into the Danish labour market, and consequently into Danish society.

In order to determine the learning outcomes for young immigrants from their attendance at Danish primary and lower secondary school, the Rockwool Foundation Research Unit contacted the Danish PISA Consortium to arrange a special PISA survey. The results of this survey were presented in a book published in 2007 by the University Press of Southern Denmark entitled *PISA Etnisk 2005* (PISA Ethnic 2005), edited by Niels Egelund and myself. This special PISA survey made possible in-depth analyses of school-pupils' performance, including the performance of pupils from non-Western backgrounds.

The current paper makes further use of this very rich PISA dataset from Denmark to investigate how the level of ethnic concentration in a school influences cognitive outcomes for both immigrants and native Danish children. Later this year, a book to be published in Danish by Gyldendal will present an overview of the entire Research Unit project on the relationship of young non-Western immigrants to the Danish educational system: *Indvandrerne og det danske uddannelsessystem. Holdninger og resultater* (Immigrants and the Danish educational system. Attitudes and results), ed. Torben Tranæs.

I would like to take this opportunity to thank Peter Jensen and Astrid Würtz Rasmussen for their major contribution to the project as a whole. I also owe my warmest thanks to the staff of the Rockwool Foundation and their Board of Directors, to Tom Kähler, the Chairman of the Board, and to Elin Schmidt, Managing Director of the Foundation, for their cooperation on this project. As always, the work on the project has been carried out in complete academic independence from the Rockwool Foundation; however, without the financial resources that the Foundation has made available, the project would not have been possible. On page 7, the authors express their thanks to a number of other people who have provided help in the preparation of this paper.

Copenhagen, August 2008 *Torben Tranæs*

Contents

Immigrant and Native Children's Cognitive Outcomes and the Effect of Ethnic Concentration in Danish Schools*

Peter Jensen† Astrid Würtz Rasmussen‡

Abstract

This paper uses a unique and very rich PISA dataset from Denmark to investigate how the ethnic concentration in the school influences cognitive outcomes for both immigrant and native Danish children. We find that immigrant children from non-Western countries have lower reading test scores than native Danish children, and that children in schools with a high ethnic concentration score significantly lower in the reading test than children in schools with a low ethnic concentration. These results are fairly robust across estimation methods. Immigrant children's lower cognitive outcome is related to the ethnic concentration in the schools they attend and their relatively low socioeconomic status. Instrumenting for ethnic concentration reveals that even after taking into consideration that individuals may sort across neighborhoods, ethnic concentration in the school and the child's own ethnicity are still important factors in determining the child's cognitive outcome. However, the negative effect of ethnic concentration in the school is only significant for the native Danish children. Finally, there is a strong positive effect on the children's cognitive outcome of speaking Danish at home.

JEL Classification: I21, J15.
Keywords: Immigrants, ethnic concentration, child outcomes.

*We would like to thank Nina Smith, Nabanita Datta Gupta, Leslie S. Stratton, Helena Skyt-Nielsen, Beatrice S. Rangvid, Anna Piil Damm, Eskild Heinesen, and Regina Riphahn for helpful suggestions. Furthermore, comments from participants at the CIM/AKF-workshop in Nyborg and the DGPE workshop in Ebeltoft are greatly appreciated. We also would like to thank Pia Elisabeth Kristensen, Ulrik Brandt Jørgensen, and Christina Bjerg for their highly competent research assistance. Finally, we thank the Rockwool Foundation Research Unit for providing the data. The usual disclaimer applies.

†CIM and Department of Economics, Aarhus School of Business, University of Aarhus. E-mail: pje@asb.dk

‡CIM and Department of Economics, Aarhus School of Business, University of Aarhus. E-mail: awu@asb.dk

1 Introduction

The share of immigrant children in schools is increasing in many Western countries. In general, the number of immigrants is increasing in most Western countries and therefore the number of immigrant children is increasing as well. Immigrants tend to choose housing around the big cities, which leads to an over-representation of immigrants in the schools in the big cities. Furthermore, parents of native children sometimes move their children to a private school with few immigrant children if there are many immigrant children at the local district school. This imbalance of native and immigrant children in schools might be a problem, since the school performance of immigrant children is often found to be poor compared to that of native children. Recently, a number of studies have examined immigrant children's cognitive outcomes, and the typical finding of these studies is that immigrant children have a disadvantage (Ammermüller, 2007; Entorf and Lauk, 2006; and Schnepf, 2007). Several reasons for the poor performance of immigrant children may exist: language skills, socioeconomic background, and school factors. Many of these explanations have been investigated in the literature, but relatively little evidence is available on the effects of going to school with many immigrant peers. The ethnic concentration of the school may influence the cognitive outcomes of both immigrant children and native children.

The aim of this paper is to analyze the effect of ethnic concentration in schools on the cognitive outcomes of children. We use a unique and very rich PISA dataset from Denmark. In these data, the cognitive outcomes of the children are measured by the PISA test score for reading abilities. Most of the children are tested in 9th grade, i.e. just before they make the decision as to whether to enroll in high school or whether to start working full-time in the labor market. We first investigate the extent to which immigrant children perform worse than native Danish children, and then we provide various explanations for this relationship, including socioeconomic background and school factors. The focus of this study will be on the effects of ethnic concentration in the schools and the children's own background.

One question that arises in investigating the effect of ethnic concentration is whether this effect is a causal effect or whether it is the result of a selection process. A given school may have a high ethnic concentration because the parents of the immigrant children have decided to live in a neighborhood with many immigrants. To deal with this problem, we use an instrument for ethnic concentration in the school: the ethnic concentration in a larger geographical area. This instrument only influences the PISA test scores through the influence of the residential choice on the ethnic concentration in the school. It does not by itself directly affect the test scores, and hence it allows us to estimate the effect of ethnic concentration correcting for the possible endogeneity.

In the empirical analysis, we show that immigrant children from non-Western countries tend to have a lower cognitive outcome than native Danish children. These results are fairly robust across estimation methods. The lower outcome of immigrant children is related to the ethnic concentration in the schools that the children attend. It is also clear from the estimation results that the low socioeconomic status of the immigrants is even more important than the ethnic concentration in schools. Instrumenting for ethnic concentration reveals that after taking into consideration that individuals sort across neighborhoods, ethnic concentration in the school and the child's own ethnicity are still important factors in determining the child's cognitive outcome. However, the negative effect of ethnic concentration in the school is only significant for the native Danish children.

Since education is a very important precondition for the integration of immigrants into the labor market, these results may have important implications for the future integration efforts of immigrants into the Danish labor market. In addition, Denmark has one of the most expensive educational systems in the world. It is therefore in itself important to target policy efforts and resources where they have an effect, especially with respect to optimizing inputs into schooling. We will discuss policy implications further in the concluding section of the paper.

The remainder of this paper is structured as follows. In Section 2, we briefly review the literature and discuss some of the determinants of cognitive outcomes. Section 3 introduces the three different estimation methods and Section 4 describes the data used in the analysis. Estimation results are provided in Section 5 and, finally, Section 6 concludes.

2 Literature Review

There are several possible explanations why immigrant and native children do not have the same educational outcomes. The children's cognitive outcomes may be affected by a variety of factors such as the characteristics of the neighborhood where they live and the characteristics of the peers with whom they go to school. In the literature, these effects are referred to as neighborhood effects and peer effects, respectively. Family background, values, and tradition for prioritizing school work will probably also affect the children's cognitive outcomes. Further, resources may vary between schools and have an impact on the children's outcomes. There can, for instance, be a variation in teacher quality, teacher/student ratio, class size, and quality of books. The effects of these school-related factors are referred to as school effects.

Most of the literature on the poor school performance of immigrant children focuses on their disadvantaged socioeconomic background. There is, however, a rapidly growing literature on peer effects, and some of this research addresses immigrant school performance. Further, the literature on neighborhood effects often focuses on immigrants. The literature which examines the effect of school environment on child performance is by contrast rather sparse, particularly in its analysis of ethnic concentration. It is this latter literature that we want to contribute to.

Socioeconomic status and family background are often found to be very important factors behind the poor school performance of immigrant children. This is the case in the study by Ammermüller (2007), who uses PISA data for Germany to investigate the differences between immigrant children and native German children. A similar analysis with the same conclusion is performed by Rangvid (2007), who uses a special PISA dataset for the city of Copenhagen. Schnepf (2007) examines differences in educational achievement between immigrants and natives across ten countries, also using PISA data, and she finds that for the five continental European countries (Germany, Switzerland, France, the Netherlands and Sweden) the differences are explained predominantly by different family backgrounds.

Several recent studies have addressed the issue of peer effects, see e.g. Hoxby

(2000), Hanushek et al. (2003), Entorf and Lauk (2008), and Ammermüller and Pischke (2006), and it is argued that the mix of students in the child's class may create or shape incentives or disincentives for studying. Typically, it is found that peer achievement has a positive effect on each student's achievement, but not necessarily the same effects for different groups. Much of the US literature is focused on the effects of white and black students, but such racial effects are also ethnicity effects of a sort. Hanushek et al. (2003) find that the racial composition of schools has an effect for black students, but not for white students. In contrast to this, Hoxby (2000) finds that peer effects primarily work within the racial groups, i.e. black peers have an influence on black students and white peers have an influence on white students. More generally, peer effects in relation to the poor school performance of immigrant children have been investigated by Entorf and Lauk (2008), who use PISA data for a number of countries. They find dominant and highly significant peer effects, and irrespective of whether immigrants or natives are considered, the direct influence of the native peer group achievement is larger than the direct influence of the immigrant peer group.

Closely related to the issue of peer influence is the issue of neighborhood effects. Borjas (1995) has provided a very illuminating discussion of this in relation to ethnicity. He investigates how the skills of immigrant children depend on the mean skills of the immigrant group (the ethnic capital) in the neighborhood, and he finds that the human capital accumulation is restrained for the less skilled groups of immigrants. A recent study of Sweden by Grönqvist (2006) specifically looks at the impact on immigrant children's educational attainment from growing up in an ethnic enclave. His evidence suggests that the size of the ethnic enclave negatively affects the children's educational attainment.

To illustrate the relevance of Borjas' arguments in the Danish case, we provide some simple evidence in Figure 1. Clearly, one mechanism through which neighborhood effects may work is that children's cognitive outcome may be affected by the role models where they live, the so-called neighborhood effects. One can easily imagine that if a child grows up in a neighborhood dominated by individuals with a low socioeconomic status, then the effect on the child may be negative because the child cannot mirror itself in positive role models. The figure shows that the employment rate is lower among immigrants from non-Western countries compared to native Danes,[1] and that especially the share of non-Western immigrants not in the labor force is much higher than for native Danes.[2] Even though the figure shows national outcomes, it illustrates that if neighborhood effects are important for determining child outcomes, then the composition of the neighborhood in terms of immigrants and native Danes is potentially very important.

[1] We define immigrant children as children born outside Denmark and whose parents are foreign citizens. Further, children born in Denmark, but where neither of the parents is both a Danish citizen *and* born in Denmark, are also defined as immigrants. Non-Western immigrants are immigrants mainly from Turkey, Libya, Iraq, Iran, Pakistan, Somalia, Vietnam, Morocco, Afghanistan, and Former Yugoslavia.

[2] Immigrants from Western countries tend to have a socioeconomic status much closer to that of native Danes. The difference between 2nd generation immigrants from Western countries and native Danes is minor, whereas the difference between 1st generation immigrants from Western countries and native Danes is somewhat larger than but not as large as for immigrants from non-Western countries. These numbers are not shown here but are available from the authors upon request.

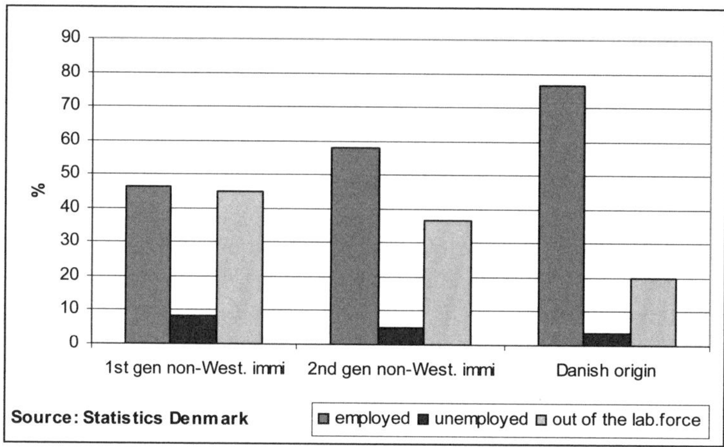

Figure 1: Percentages of individuals aged 16-64 who are employed, unemployed, or out of the labor force within 1st generation immigrants from non-Western countries, 2nd generation immigrants from non-Western countries, and individuals of Danish origin, Denmark 2005.

The evidence on the effects of school segregation (in particular, of the ethnic concentration in the school) is rather sparse. However, this is the literature most relevant for our study, since our contribution falls into this area. Schnepf (2007) includes a measure of the immigrants' distribution across schools in her analysis, and using PISA data for ten countries she finds mixed evidence on the effects of ethnic concentration. For two countries (Australia and Canada), a higher concentration seems even to improve pupils' educational achievement, whereas for some countries (the Netherlands, Sweden, the UK, and the US) it is unimportant. For four countries (Switzerland, Germany, New Zealand, and France), a high ethnic concentration has a negative impact on achievement. It should, however, be noted that she uses a relatively crude measure of ethnic concentration and that the analysis is only performed by simple OLS estimations. The effects of ethnic concentration in the school have also been addressed in sociology, where Szulkin and Jonsson (2007) analyze to what extent ethnic concentration in Swedish schools has consequences for pupils' school achievements. Their analysis suggests that ethnic concentration in schools has a negative effect on grades, in particular for immigrant children and to a lesser degree for native children. Robustness checks for biased estimates support the main findings. Finally, a preliminary analysis to the present one has been performed by Jensen and Smith (2007). They also find that ethnic concentration in Danish schools has a negative impact on children's cognitive outcomes.

Turning to methodological issues, the literature suggests that there are several possible endogeneity problems to be aware of. First, there is a potential problem with determining neighborhood effects. Ethnic concentration in the schools may be endogenous because individuals sort into neighborhoods because they want (or do not want) to live in a ghetto area. Since we do not have random assignment to housing in general in Denmark, we have to consider this potential endogeneity problem in the empirical analysis.[3]

Further, when investigating children's cognitive outcomes, one has to recognize that peer effects may also be endogenous. The peer group can be the result of individual choices, e.g. based on unobserved school quality. Entorf and Lauk (2008) give an overview of the possible effects in relation to the school performance of immigrant children. In addition, different school types are also likely to determine the size of peer effects.[4] In many cases, it is difficult to separate neighborhood effects and peer effects, since most children attend schools in the proximity of their residence. Parents' housing decisions may also simultaneously depend on choices about preferred neighborhood and school.

Lastly, as Hoxby (2000) emphasizes, school resources are probably endogenous since they are not randomly allocated to municipalities, schools or students. Therefore, parents may choose housing based on schools in the area. Furthermore, school administrators, teachers and politicians affect school resources by allocating more resources to schools with many "weak" students, or by creating smaller classes for weak students.

Omitted background variables related to outcomes from schooling might be correlated with school resources and cause bias (up or down) in single equation estimates. Hanushek et al. (2003) argue that issues of omitted and mismeasured variables are likely to be more important than for example whether peer interactions are simultaneously determined. Omitted variables bias can be addressed using instruments of class size, teacher/student ratio, etc.; see e.g. Browning and Heinesen (2007). Another way to deal with omitted variables bias is by including a large set of controls, and this is the approach we will take.

Todd and Wolpin (2003) emphasize that for an empirical investigation of children's educational outcomes one optimally needs information on both family and school inputs, current and past. This ensures a correct specification of the child's cognitive achievement production function when considering child development as a cumulative process depending on the history of family and school inputs as well as on inherited endowments.

The early childhood development (ECD) model and the education production function (EPF) model are production function models often used for the study of child cognitive achievement. The ECD model is used when short-term development is the focus of the model for child development, while the EPF model is used when focus is on longer term effects, e.g. for school-age children. In many studies, ECD or EPF models are estimated without having a dataset with sufficiently rich information. In ECD studies, the datasets lack information on school inputs, whereas in EPF studies

[3]For a small group of individuals, refugees, we have seen random assignment to housing as a result of the government's refugee placement policy in the period 1986 to 1998. This potential instrument cannot be used in our analysis since there are too few refugee children from the relevant countries who have immigrated in the specified time period. The method of using this "quasi experiment" to find exogenous variation in residence for refugees has been used by e.g. Edin et al. (2003) for Sweden and Damm (2009) for Denmark.

[4]In general, it may be very difficult to identify different types of peer effects because of the "reflection problem"; see Manski (1993). However, the analyses in the present paper do not attempt to identify the different types of peer effects separately.

there is often little information available on family inputs. Furthermore, there seems to be a lack of consensus over which variables to include in the different specifications. This implies that researchers working on the same data source can find completely opposite effects of e.g. maternal employment on children's cognitive achievement; see also Todd and Wolpin (2003).

The data sources that will be used in this study suffer to a much smaller degree from these problems with lack of information on either family or school inputs. The availability of register information ensures that the data contain information on families back to the year of a child's birth, and the surveys contain extra background information not included in registers. Furthermore, some school information is included in the registers and the surveys. Using a dataset with such rich information will improve identification, reduce omitted variables bias and allow for several different estimation methods. We take a closer look at these methods in the next section.

3 Empirical Model

To address the question of whether immigrant children's cognitive outcomes are lower than those of native Danish children and to investigate whether ethnic concentration in schools affects children's outcomes, we employ three different estimation methods. First, we use a simple OLS analysis, even though we risk finding biased estimates. This provides a reference point for the other estimation methods. Second, an instrumental variables (IV) analysis is used, where an instrument for ethnic concentration in schools is included. Third, a school fixed effect analysis (FE) removes observed and unobserved fixed school effects that may affect children in the same school in the same way.[5] For the purpose of identifying causal effects on child outcome, the latter two methods are appropriate. In general, an extensive set of family, school, and background variables from both the survey and the registers is included in the estimations to reduce omitted variables bias.

Our approach is based on the EPF model as defined by Todd and Wolpin (2003). The general (or cumulative) expression for the empirical model is given as

$$T_{ija} = T_a \left[F_{ij}(a), S_{ij}(a), \mu_{ij0}, \varepsilon_{ija} \right], \tag{1}$$

where T_{ija} is a measure of achievement for child i from household j at age a, F is a vector containing the history of parent-supplied inputs up to the given age a, and S is a vector containing the history of school-supplied inputs. μ_{ij0} is the child's (unobserved) endowed ability, and ε_{ija} is a measurement error in test scores. The impact of inputs and genetic endowment is allowed to depend on the age of the child in this general specification. For consistent estimation, information on both contemporaneous and historical family and school inputs is needed.

In the empirical analysis, we assume that T_{ija} can be expressed as a linear function of the explanatory variables. Simplifying the notation, the OLS regression is the following:

$$T_i = \beta_0 + \beta_1 F_i + \beta_2 \tilde{S}_i + \beta_3 \breve{S}_i + \varepsilon_i, \tag{2}$$

[5]We would also like to use FE on individuals to remove individuals' unobserved heterogeneity, but since we only have one PISA test score per child, this method is not feasible with our data. Further, we do not have school class indicators, so we cannot do FE estimations within schools.

where school inputs are split into ethnic concentration in the school, $\breve{S}_i$, and all other school variables, $\tilde{S}_i$. Some of the variables included are only available for the year the child is tested, whereas information such as parental employment and work experience is known back in time. Assuming that the error term, ε_i, is not correlated with the explanatory variables ensures consistent OLS estimates.

In the IV analysis, we recognize that ethnic concentration in schools, $\breve{S}_i$, might be endogenous. The reason is that most children attend schools that are geographically close to their neighborhood,[6] and ethnic concentration in the neighborhood is most likely not random. Parents may sort across neighborhoods. We therefore introduce an instrument, Z_i, for ethnic concentration in schools. The instrument follows Dustmann and Preston (2001) in using ethnic concentration in a larger geographical area as an instrument for local ethnic concentration. If mobility is geographically limited by employment and family history, and ethnic concentration in the larger geographical area does not directly affect child outcomes, this seems to be a good instrument for local ethnic concentration. We test the strength of the instrument and argue for validity in Section 5.2. If the instrument is weak, we may encounter problems with the estimator, since standard errors using IV methods tend to be large, especially for weak instruments; see e.g. Wooldridge (2002), Bound et al. (1995), and Staiger and Stock (1997). This does not seem to be a big problem in our analysis.

In the IV analysis, the endogenous variable is first regressed on the instruments and all exogenous variables in the model using OLS,

$$\breve{S}_i = \delta_0 + \delta_1 F_i + \delta_2 \tilde{S}_i + \delta_3 Z_i + r_i \tag{3}$$

and thereafter (inserting Equation (3) in Equation (2)) one estimates

$$T_i = \alpha_0 + \alpha_1 F_i + \alpha_2 \tilde{S}_i + \lambda_1 Z_i + \nu_i \tag{4}$$

by OLS, where $\nu_i = \varepsilon_i + \beta_3 r_i$, $\alpha_j = \beta_j + \beta_3 \delta_j$, and $\lambda_1 = \beta_3 \delta_3$. If the instrument is truly exogenous, we get consistent OLS estimates in the second stage.

Finally, when taking school fixed effects into account, we remove all observable and unobservable factors that are fixed and common to children in the same school. This approach enables us to control for such factors as resources per child, teacher quality, and the school principal at the school. We also control for the ethnic concentration in the school, since this factor is fixed within schools. However, we cannot determine the true causal effect of school-immigrant concentration, as all fixed school factors are included in the same term, γ. The following equation is estimated:

$$T_{is} = \beta_0 + \beta_1 F_{is} + \beta_2 \tilde{S}_{is} + \gamma_s + \varepsilon_{is},$$

where s denotes the school and γ_s is the fixed effect in school s.

[6] Based on address of residence, the child belongs to a certain public district school. In principle, parents have had the freedom to choose their child's school since May 2005, but children can only go to a school other than the district school if the chosen school has room for extra students. Since our data were collected from February to April in 2000 and 2005, free choice of school is not a concern for us. Moreover, parents have always been able to send their children to a private school, provided they were willing to pay for it.

4 Data

The data used for studying children's cognitive outcomes is a unique combination of PISA survey data and Danish administrative register data. PISA is the acronym for the OECD Programme for International Student Assessment.

The survey data consists of the Danish subsample of the PISA study from the year 2000 which is combined with a special Danish PISA study from 2005 in which there is an oversampling of immigrants. The PISA study from 2005 will be referred to as PISA-Ethnic in the following. The children in PISA-Ethnic are given exactly the same cognitive test as the children participating in the PISA-2000 study. For information on the PISA-2000 study, see OECD (2002).

A personal identification number has been recorded for the children participating in the PISA studies, and this allows us to combine PISA information with register data from Statistics Denmark. This gives us information on the child and his/her parents from birth to the year 2005 (2000 for the children participating in PISA-2000). Furthermore, PISA children have answered questionnaires about their family background, and school principals have answered a questionnaire about school resources, etc. This information is also linked to the child. We include a wide variety of these background variables from questionnaires and registers in our models to decrease possible omitted variables bias.

The dependent variable in this study is the child's PISA reading score.[7] OECD has standardized the mean score across all OECD countries participating in PISA-2000 to 500, with a standard deviation of 100. The Danish average test score in reading is just below the OECD mean. PISA-2000 focuses on children's reading abilities but also tests some of the children in mathematics and science. We focus on the reading score, since all children are tested in reading, and we are able directly to compare reading scores from the two studies, since the cognitive test for PISA-Ethnic children is the same as for PISA-2000 children. One might argue that it would be more fair to use the mathematics score as the measure of cognitive outcome, as mathematics is not as biased against immigrants as reading. On the other hand, reading skills are very important for future school and labor market opportunities, so it is a relevant skill to investigate.

The distribution of test scores for immigrant children is quite different from the distribution for native Danes. Figure 2 shows that reading test scores for immigrant children in general are much lower than for native Danes. The distribution for native

[7]Two types of test scores are provided in the PISA studies: the "plausible values" (PV) and "Weighted Likelihood Estimator" (WLE) scores. We use the WLE score in our analyses, since we are investigating individual outcomes. For the purpose of comparing between countries the PV score is recommended, see OECD (2002). The WLE score is calculated by the ACER institute in Australia, which is responsible for all PISA analyses. WLE scores are not simple observed test statistics but instead based on estimated models for all countries participating in the analysis under study. The test scores from PISA-2000 and PISA-Ethnic are calibrated in the same way and are therefore directly comparable. Standard deviations are calculated as simple standard deviations which do not take into account that each WLE score has been calculated, i.e. is not directly observed. In regressions and for statistical tests, we will use the PISA test scores *as if* they were observed test scores. This is the only practical solution for performing statistical analyses using this type of data, and it is the same method used in other Danish and international studies. For a critical discussion of the PISA measures and an evaluation of the "fairness" of the test, see Allerup (2005).

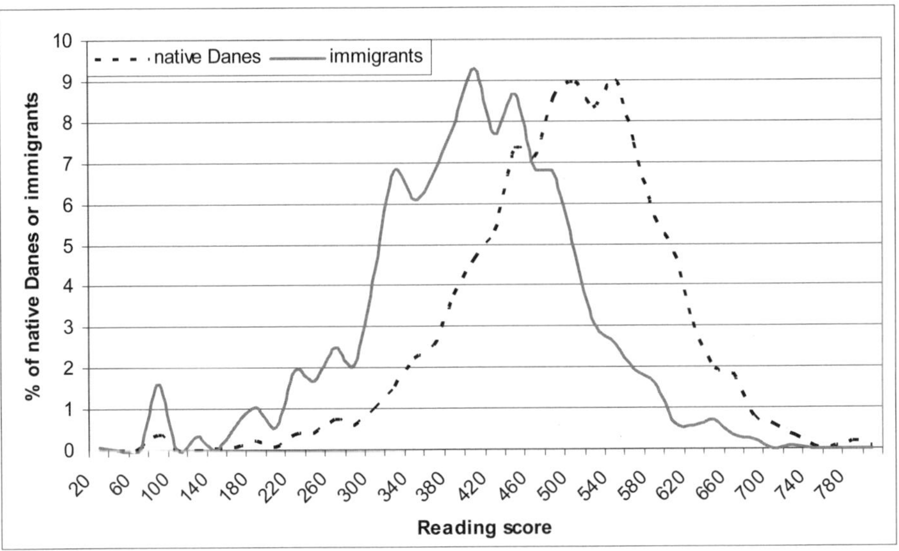

Figure 2: Distribution of reading test scores for native Danes and immigrant children.

Danes is more centered around (and above) the OECD defined mean of 500. The difference in distributions might be attributed to different socioeconomic backgrounds of the two groups or to school factors. We investigate this further in the empirical analysis in Section 5.

The sampling criteria are slightly different for the two surveys. PISA-2000 consists of a random sample of schools in Denmark, and from these sampled schools 15-year-old children are chosen in order to make the sample representative for Danish 15-year-olds. Since the purpose of PISA-Ethnic is to oversample immigrant children, the way schools are chosen for participation in PISA-Ethnic is a little different. All schools in Denmark are ranked according to the number of immigrants in the school in 2003, and then the schools from the top of the distribution are chosen. In other words, the schools are not randomly chosen and the children in these schools are more often immigrants. This implies that the number of immigrants is big enough for making statistical analyses based on ethnicity. The different sampling is apparent in Figure 3, which shows the distribution of ethnic concentration in schools in PISA-2000 and PISA-Ethnic. Most of the schools in the PISA-Ethnic sample have less than 40% non-Western immigrants but we also see that some schools have more than 90% non-Western immigrants. In PISA-2000, most of the schools have less than 5% ethnic concentration.

All children participating in PISA-2000 are 15 years old. The PISA-Ethnic sample, on the other hand, is collected from students in the 9th grade and the children are not sampled by age. Therefore, some children in the PISA-Ethnic sample are older than 15. 80% of PISA-Ethnic children are 15 years old, 95% are 15 or 16 years old. We only keep 15- and 16-year-old children from the PISA-Ethnic sample but note that

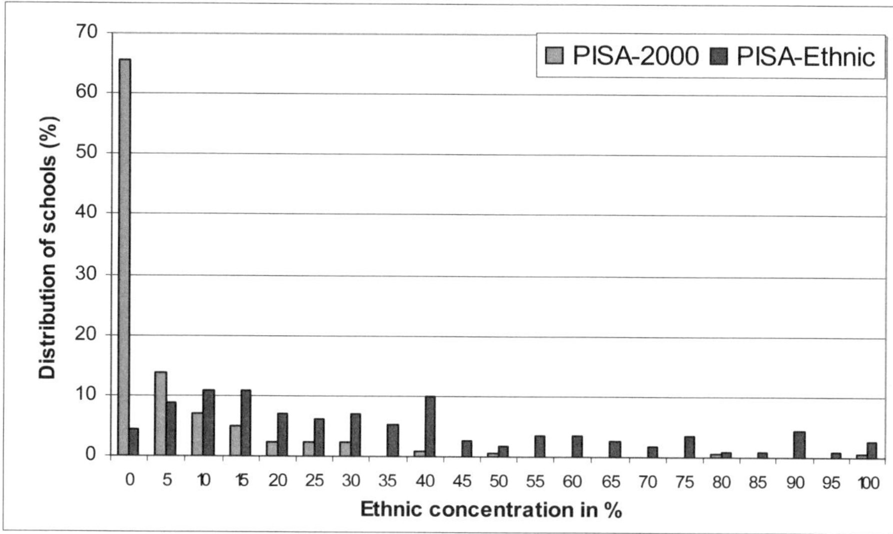

Figure 3: Distribution of ethnic concentration in schools, shown separately for the PISA-2000 and PISA-Ethnic samples. Ethnic concentration is shown in groups of 5%.

this might bias test scores slightly.[8] It should further be mentioned that the drop-out rate in Danish schools is very low. Statistics from the Danish Ministry of Education show that the drop-out rate among children in 8th to 10th grade is only about 4%.

When PISA-2000 and PISA-Ethnic are pooled, we end up with a unique sample of children where a high share of the children have non-native Danish backgrounds. We also have a lot of native Danes in the pooled sample, mainly from the original PISA-2000 sample. We therefore have information that allows us to make analyses which are not possible in most other countries, for example we can investigate the effect of having immigrant peers. For these analyses to be valid for the pooled PISA-2000 and PISA-Ethnic dataset, we have to assume that the mechanisms determining cognitive outcomes did not change over time and that there are no substantial cohort effects beyond a mean shift. This is confirmed by a Chow test on natives, which shows that the determinants of cognitive outcomes are identical in 2000 and 2005.[9]

In the estimation dataset, we keep immigrants from non-Western countries but drop immigrants from Western countries. The latter group is dropped since they

[8] In 2000, a separate survey was completed among a large group of 16-year-olds in Denmark. They were given exactly the same PISA test as the 15-year-olds, and it turned out that the results were a little better but still very similar to the results for 15-year-old Danes; see Andersen et al. (2001). In our sample with many immigrant children, we might instead find that keeping 16-year-olds in the sample will bias test scores downwards. These older children may actually be a selected group in the sense that they have delayed schooling because of language difficulties, for example. Descriptive evidence confirms that 16-year-olds in the PISA-Ethnic sample are 1st generation immigrants to a larger degreee than they are 2nd generation immigrants.

[9] This is tested without clustering on schools, though. The F-statistic is 0.8377.

only constitute 1.5% of the PISA-Ethnic sample and 1.2% of the PISA-2000 sample. Further, they have very different characteristics than the non-Western immigrants, as many of the Western immigrants come from the other Nordic countries or from Northern Europe. The comparison group in the analyses is children from "ethnic Danish" schools defined as schools in which up to 5% of the children in 9th grade are non-Western immigrants. 47% of the children in the PISA-2000 sample do not have any non-Western immigrant schoolmates, and 67% have 5% or less. Only 4% of the PISA-Ethnic sample attend schools with up to 5% ethnic concentration.

Table 1 shows means and standard errors for all variables included in the analysis. For comparison, means for individuals in the PISA-2000 and PISA-Ethnic samples are shown separately along with means for the estimation sample, the pooled PISA-2000 and PISA-Ethnic sample.[10]

Most of the mean values are significantly different between the PISA-2000 and PISA-Ethnic samples, as shown by asterisks in Table 1. For example, the PISA test score in reading is much lower for individuals in the PISA-Ethnic sample than for children in the PISA-2000 sample. The ethnic concentration is of course much higher in PISA-Ethnic children's schools and so is the share of schoolmates living in "problem housing estates". The definition of a problem housing estate is a housing estate which has received money from the "Government's City Committee" (Regeringens Byudvalg) in 1994 for social activities or for hiring resident consultants. The problem housing estates are aggregated into 5 groups based on the severity of social problems. All 5 groups are categorized as problem housing estates and they include approximately 200,000 individuals in total.[11] Immigrants tend to live in non-profit rental housing and mainly this type of housing is categorized as a problem housing estate. We further notice that ethnic concentration in the county and the commuting area is higher for PISA-Ethnic children, which indicates that they often live around the big cities.

16% of children in the PISA-Ethnic sample are 16 years old, whereas all children in PISA-2000 are 15 years old because of the sampling technique. Since 1st generation immigrants in 9th grade tend to be older than 2nd generation immigrants, we control for this in the analysis by including separate indicators identifying 1st and 2nd generation immigrants. Further, PISA-Ethnic children's parents have weaker characteristics than PISA-2000 parents with respect to length of education, occupation, labor market attachment, family gross income,[12] and work experience. This might be one explanation for PISA-Ethnic children's lower test scores, and we therefore control for these background characteristics in the empirical analysis.

The study environment for PISA-2000 and PISA-Ethnic children is quite similar.

[10]Further, means and standard deviations separately by ethnicity are shown in Tables 7 and 8 in Appendix B.

[11]The final aggregation is based on a "problem-indicator" which depends on the share of residents from ethnic minorities, the unemployment rate, the share of inhabitants aged 18 to 66 who receive cash assistance from the municipality but without being listed as unemployed, the share of inhabitants aged 18 to 66 who are early retired, the share of households with single parents, the average disposable income per person in the housing estate compared to the average disposable income per person in the municipality (individuals aged 18 to 66), and the size of the housing estate. For more on the definition and grouping of problem housing estates, see Appendix 1 in Hummelgaard et al. (1997).

[12]Gross income is deflated to 2005 DKK.

	Pooled sample		PISA-2000		PISA-Ethnic	
	mean	std.dev.	mean	std.dev.	mean	std.dev.
WLE-test score, reading	484.18	104.92	498.03*	97.92	469.51	109.99
ethnic concentration	17.45	21.11	5.63*	10.24	29.98	22.40
ethnic conc. 0-5 (0/1)	0.37	0.48	0.67*	0.47	0.04	0.21
ethnic conc. 5-25 (0/1)	0.38	0.48	0.27*	0.44	0.49	0.50
ethnic conc. 25-50 (0/1)	0.17	0.38	0.05*	0.22	0.30	0.46
ethnic conc. 50-100 (0/1)	0.08	0.28	0.00*	0.06	0.17	0.38
share sch.mates in probl. hous. estate	12.38	20.44	4.31*	10.09	20.92	24.72
ethnic conc. in the county	5.30	2.46	4.04*	1.80	6.65	2.36
ethnic conc. in the commuting area	4.87	2.86	3.93*	2.35	5.86	3.02
non-West. immigrant (0/1)	0.17	0.37	0.05*	0.22	0.29	0.46
Danish origin (0/1)	0.83	0.37	0.95*	0.22	0.71	0.46
1st gen. immigrant (0/1)	0.08	0.27	0.03*	0.18	0.13	0.33
2nd gen. immigrant (0/1)	0.09	0.29	0.02*	0.13	0.17	0.37
years since migration	14.48	2.09	14.62*	1.85	14.33	2.32
girl (0/1)	0.50	0.50	0.50	0.50	0.51	0.50
student 16 y.o. (0/1)	0.08	0.27	0.00*	0.00	0.16	0.36
father's length of edu. (years)	11.81	3.24	11.99*	2.87	11.61	3.58
mother's length of edu. (years)	11.50	3.45	11.71*	3.05	11.29	3.81
family gross income (/DKK 100,000)	4.90	3.98	5.19*	4.51	4.62	3.37
father's occ., self-empl. (0/1)	0.10	0.30	0.13*	0.34	0.08	0.26
father's occ., high level (0/1)	0.19	0.39	0.21*	0.41	0.17	0.38
father's occ., medium/low level (0/1)	0.55	0.50	0.56*	0.50	0.53	0.50
father's occ., not working (0/1)	0.16	0.37	0.10*	0.30	0.22	0.42
mother's occ., self-empl. (0/1)	0.04	0.19	0.05*	0.21	0.03	0.17
mother's occ., high level (0/1)	0.12	0.33	0.14*	0.35	0.11	0.31
mother's occ., medium/low level (0/1)	0.62	0.49	0.66*	0.47	0.58	0.49
mother's occ., not working (0/1)	0.22	0.41	0.15*	0.36	0.29	0.45
father's work exp. (years)	17.68	9.03	19.14*	7.87	16.11	9.88
mother's work exp. (years)	13.78	8.35	14.99*	7.39	12.49	9.09
speak Danish at home (0/1)	0.87	0.34	0.94*	0.23	0.79	0.41
number of siblings	1.99	1.35	1.90*	1.28	2.09	1.42
index: cultural possessions (-1.65;1.15)	-0.17	0.99	-0.12*	0.97	-0.22	1.00
more than 500 books (0/1)	0.12	0.33	0.13	0.33	0.11	0.32
quiet place to study (0/1)	0.84	0.36	0.87*	0.33	0.81	0.39
living in problem housing estate (0/1)	0.12	0.32	0.04*	0.19	0.20	0.40
private school (0/1)	0.15	0.35	0.23*	0.42	0.04	0.20
number of students	484.36	204.64	424.12*	207.62	564.70	170.16
number of students per class	20.06	2.16	19.92*	2.05	20.19	2.25
teacher/student ratio	0.04	0.08	0.04*	0.09	0.04	0.07
index: time spent on homework (1-4)	2.58	0.61	2.59	0.61	2.58	0.61
obs	7420		3817		3603	

Note: * indicates that the mean value is significantly different in PISA-2000 and PISA-Ethnic.

Table 1: Means for all variables included in estimations.

The number of books in the household is not significantly different but the availability of a quiet place to study is a bit higher for PISA-2000 children. There are big differences between households in the number of siblings and in the language spoken. Fewer PISA-Ethnic children speak Danish with their parents, which is not surprising.

Finally, there are systematic differences between PISA-2000 and PISA-Ethnic children's schools, which makes it likely that the school FE analysis provides new information. PISA-Ethnic children attend bigger schools, the schools are more often public schools,[13] and the number of students per class is somewhat higher. The teacher/student ratio is significantly different between the two samples according to the statistical test, but the difference is not huge. The amount of time the children spend doing homework is not significantly different between the two samples according to the homework index, which takes values from 1 to 4, where 4 indicates that the child spends a lot of time on homework.

The variables in this study originate from either administrative registers or the PISA surveys. Information from the registers include ethnic concentration in schools, counties, and the commuting area. Information about problem housing estates is also from the registers along with information about ethnicity of the child, years since migration, gender, and age. The indices on cultural possessions and time spent on homework are from the surveys, along with information on siblings,[14] books in the household, and whether the child has a quiet place to study. The school information primarily stems from the school questionnaire, but the information about number of students per class is from the administrative register. Parental background information such as the level of education, occupation, income, and work experience is from the registers. This implies that the quality of this information is lower for parents of immigrants than for native Danes, because work experience etc. from the country of origin is not recorded in the Danish administrative registers. Thus, in the empirical analysis the indicator variables for ethnicity might capture some of this omitted information. In practice, this might not be important, as the coefficients of parental work experience are insignificant in the estimations, and, more importantly, there is not a problem in relation to interpreting the results for ethnic concentration as these are on the school or county level. Furthermore, what is measured in the registers is likely what is relevant for the parents' job opportunities in Denmark, since this is what a Danish employer can see documentation for.

5 Estimation Results

In the following subsections, estimation results from the OLS, IV, and FE analyses are reported and discussed.[15]

[13]The high number of PISA-2000 children attending private schools reflects, that many (native) Danes attend boarding schools in 9th grade instead of going to the public district school. Most of the boarding schools are specialized in e.g. sports, music, theater, etc.

[14]If sibling information is missing in the survey, we use information from the registers instead.

[15]If one of the explanatory variables is missing for an individual, we employ the commonly used practise of adding an indicator variable with the value 1 and changing the value of the original variable to 0 in order not to lose the observation. The coefficients of these indicator variables are not included in any of the tables below. Generally, there are about the same level of missing observations for immigrant children as for native Danes.

5.1 OLS Estimation

We start out using OLS so as to have a benchmark. We realize that OLS estimates are likely to be biased when they include potentially endogenous variables, and we examine this possibility in the next subsection. All results reported in Models 1-4 in Table 2 are based on the pooled sample of children from PISA-2000 and PISA-Ethnic. The results in this and the following tables are all based on standard errors of estimated coefficients that are robust with respect to clustering within schools. This is done to avoid the so-called Moulton-bias, since some of the variables only vary at school level, such as ethnic concentration and school characteristics.[16]

The models in Table 2 add progressively more and more explanatory variables in an effort to model reading test scores. Models 1-3 include variables which, except for ethnic concentration in the school, seem to be exogenous to the dependent variable, child test score. The first model includes only information on ethnicity and gender. The second adds controls for common family background characteristics, and the third some controls for family background that are probably unique to this study. Model 4 includes more variables that are potentially endogenous to child outcome, namely whether the child lives in a problem housing estate, whether the child attends a private school, the number of students per school, the teacher/student ratio, and an index for time spent on homework. This index is probably endogenous, because the amount of time spent on homework depends on the child's ability and interest in school work. In the following, we will focus mainly on Models 1-3.

If we first look at ethnic concentration in the school, we see that a higher ethnic concentration is significantly related to lower child outcomes in the PISA reading test. This result is robust across specifications. Parental and family background information seems to explain some of the negative effect of ethnic concentration in the school, since the negative effect of ethnic concentration on the reading score decreases from Model 1 to Model 2. The negative effect of ethnic concentration is mainly driven by a negative effect in schools with a very high share of children with a non-Western background. This is seen in Appendix Table 6, where indicators for ethnic concentration between 5 and 25%, 25 and 50%, and above 50% are included in the model instead of the continuous variable for ethnic concentration. The reference category is schools with up to 5% ethnic concentration (this cut-off has been chosen since 5% roughly corresponds to one child per class). It is seen that the major reduction in test scores occurs in schools with an ethnic concentration above 50%. This result confirms the results obtained by Jensen and Smith (2007) who analyzed only the PISA-Ethnic sample, and it is also very similar to the results obtained by Szulkin and Jonsson (2007) who found that students in schools with an ethnic concentration above 40% received significantly lower grades. Including indicators for ethnic concentration instead of the continuous variable for ethnic concentration does not change the estimated coefficients of the other explanatory variables much. In addition to the specification with indicators, we also analyzed various alternative ways of introducing non-linearities in the specification of the effect of ethnic concentration. None of these alternatives (e.g. with squared or cubic terms) showed any evidence of non-linear effects of ethnic concentration. It should be noted that in these models

[16]To reduce the size of the tables, standard errors are not reported in any of the tables. It is instead reported whether coefficients are significant at the 5 or 10% level.

Explanatory variables	Model 1	Model 2	Model 3	Model 4
constant	507.16**	367.82**	331.33**	350.91**
ethnic concentration	-0.46**	-0.27**	-0.23**	-0.22**
1st gen. immigrant (0/1)	-87.87**	-20.94**	-22.47**	-26.02**
2nd gen. immigrant (0/1)	-74.86**	-7.33	-10.94*	-14.44**
years since migration	-0.98	-0.59	-0.41	-0.35
girl (0/1)	25.63**	27.64**	26.29**	25.40**
father's length of edu. (years)		3.29**	2.80**	2.71**
mother's length of edu. (years)		3.30**	2.70**	2.54**
family gross income (/DKK 100,000)		1.50**	1.18**	1.03**
father's occ., self-empl. (0/1)		0.01	-2.52	-2.09
father's occ., high level (0/1)		20.43**	14.97**	14.44**
father's occ., not working (0/1)		-0.43	-0.93	-0.83
mother's occ., self-empl. (0/1)		1.90	-1.15	0.29
mother's occ., high level (0/1)		26.75**	20.03**	20.22**
mother's occ., not working (0/1)		-6.47*	-7.75**	-7.76**
father's work exp. (years)		0.17	0.21	0.15
mother's work exp. (years)		0.17	0.01	-0.07
speak Danish at home (0/1)		35.67**	29.65**	28.45**
number of siblings		-2.52**	-2.57**	-2.25**
index: cultural possessions (-1.65;1.15)			10.80**	10.30**
more than 500 books (0/1)			10.17**	10.40**
quiet place to study (0/1)			13.70**	13.44**
living in probl. housing estate (0/1)				-7.88
private school (0/1)				-2.60
number of students				0.04**
teacher/student ratio				24.74
index: time spent on homework (1-4)				7.42**
R-squared	0.13	0.22	0.24	0.25
obs	7420	7420	7420	7420

**: significant at the 5% level, *: significant at the 10% level.

Table 2: OLS estimation results using WLE reading score as the dependent variable. Pooled sample of PISA-2000 and PISA-Ethnic.

including both immigrant and native Danish children it is possible that the ethnic concentration effects may be different for the two groups of children. Only 2% of immigrant children are in schools with an ethnic concentration below 5%, whereas this is the case for 44% of native Danish children. Only 3% of native Danish children are in schools with an ethnic concentration above 50%, whereas this is the case for 36% of immigrant children. Thus, concentration effects for high levels of concentration mainly reflect effects for immigrants, whereas effects for low levels of concentration mainly reflect effects for native Danes. At the end of this section, we report results from separate models for the two groups.

Turning to the students' ethnic background, we see that controlling for the ethnic concentration in the school, children with a non-Western background have significantly lower test scores than native Danish children, with the magnitude of the reduction smaller for a 2nd than for a 1st generation immigrant. This is probably related to the fact that the 1st generation immigrant children in many cases have not been in the Danish school system throughout their entire school-lives. They therefore might have to struggle more with language issues etc. In an effort to control for time in Denmark, we include a measure of years since migration, but find that it is statistically insignificant in every specification. This result is in contrast to the result obtained by Schnepf (2007) who finds that those immigrant pupils who have stayed longer in the country fare better than new arrivals. Once again, controlling for family background substantially reduces the magnitude of the effect of the students' own ethnicity on reading test scores. Model 1 indicates that non-Western immigrant children have test scores between 75 and 88 points below their Danish peers, whereas the reduction is only between 11 and 22 points in Model 3. One of the most important family background variables in this model is whether the child speaks Danish with the parents at home, a factor that is strongly positively related to reading scores and probably related to ethnic background as well.[17]

Furthermore, several other variables have clearly significant coefficients. A very robust result is that girls score about 26 points more in the reading test than boys. The more education and the higher income the parents have, i.e. the higher the socioeconomic status, the better the child outcome. We see in Appendix Tables 7 and 8 that immigrant children's parents tend to have less education and lower income than parents of children with a native Danish background. The parents' occupational level also seems to be important for child outcome, especially if the mother is in high-level occupation. This increases child reading score by about 20 points. On the other hand, if the mother is not working, which is dominantly the case for immigrant children, then there is a significantly negative effect on child outcome. After controlling for parental education and occupation, parental work experience has no impact on child

[17]It should be noted that this variable is defined for both immigrant children and native Danish children. It is relevant for both groups. A small proportion of the native Danish children do not speak Danish with their parents at home, either because they speak another Western language (e.g. Swedish, English, etc.) or because they speak a non-Western language, presumably because they are third generation immigrants and hence classified as Danish children. For immigrant children, about 20% speak Danish with their parents at home. In the separate analysis for immigrant children and native Danish children (see later), we still find this to be one of the most important family background variables for both groups, but not surprisingly with a stronger impact among Danish children.

outcome. PISA-Ethnic children tend to have more siblings, which might be related to the higher fraction of mothers not working. The effect on the reading score of more siblings is slightly negative.

Finally, we see that the better the study environment, i.e. the more books at home, the more cultural possessions, and the greater the availability of a quiet place to study, the better the child's reading test score. Each of these factors seems to increase the reading score by about 10 points, but at the same time reduces the coefficients to parental education, occupation, and gross income as compared to Model 2. As shown in Table 1, the number of books at home and the availability of a quiet place to study are almost the same for PISA-2000 and PISA-Ethnic children.

Including school information in Model 4 does not have a huge impact on most of the coefficients from Model 3. An index for time spent on homework is also included, and the coefficient shows that if the child spends more time on homework, then the reading score is significantly higher. As mentioned earlier, this index is likely to be endogenous, so these coefficient estimates should be regarded with some caution.

In addition to the analysis performed on the sample of all children, whether they are immigrants or natives, we have estimated the same models for the two groups of children separately. The results from these separate estimations are reported in Appendix B. In general, the results are qualitatively similar, although with some variation in the magnitudes of the coefficients. With respect to the effect of the ethnic concentration, we see that it has a somewhat stronger impact upon native Danish children than upon immigrant children. If indicators for ethnic concentration are included in the separate models instead of the continuous variable for ethnic concentration, we see that for native Danish children the major reduction in test scores occurs in schools with an ethnic concentration above 50%, whereas for immigrant children the negative effect of ethnic concentration appears already at a level of 5% ethnic concentration, while the effect is similar in magnitude for all schools with an ethnic concentration above 5%. It should be noted, however, that due to the smaller sample size none of these effects are statistically significant for immigrant children.

5.2 IV Estimation

To address the issue of the potential endogeneity of the ethnic concentration in the school caused by individuals' sorting across neighborhoods, instrumental variables can be used. A good instrument is a variable that is correlated with ethnic concentration but uncorrelated with children's educational outcome.

The instrument we propose using for ethnic concentration in the school is the ethnic concentration in a larger geographical area. This instrument is used in a similar way by Dustmann and Preston (2001). The idea is that individuals' housing decisions are endogenous locally but individuals are bound to certain larger areas because of job, family etc., so ethnic concentration in the larger geographical area is exogenous to child educational outcome. This instrument is valid if ethnic composition of larger areas is highly correlated with ethnic concentration in smaller areas but is beyond the control of individuals. For ethnic concentration in a larger geographical area we use the county. Table 3 shows the ethnic concentration in the 14 Danish counties in 2000 and 2005, and it is seen that there is a relatively large variation between counties. Bornholm has the lowest ethnic concentration with only about 1.5% individuals with

County	Eth. concentration, 2000	Eth. concentration, 2005
Copenhagen	0.078	0.097
Frederiksborg	0.047	0.057
Aarhus	0.046	0.057
Funen	0.042	0.053
Roskilde	0.042	0.052
Vejle	0.036	0.048
Western Zealand	0.036	0.046
Ribe	0.031	0.040
Ringkjoebing	0.028	0.038
Southern Jutland	0.024	0.035
Storstroem	0.025	0.034
Northern Jutland	0.024	0.032
Viborg	0.019	0.026
Bornholm	0.015	0.015

Table 3: Ethnic concentration in the Danish counties in 2000 and 2005, Western immigrants are not included. Counties are ordered by ethnic concentration in 2005.

a non-Western origin, whereas Copenhagen has the largest with 9.7% in 2005. This variable enters the model as a time-varying variable, where the values for 2000 are used for observations from PISA-2000 and the values for 2005 are used for observations from PISA-Ethnic.[18]

We also considered using the share of non-profit rental housing in the area as an instrument. This could serve as an instrument, since immigrants often live in this kind of housing. Intuitively, this instrument seems valid, since the share of non-profit rental housing in the area does not directly affect the child's educational outcome. We do not have direct information about all individuals' type of housing, but we have an indicator for whether an individual lives in a so-called problem housing estate, as described in Section 4. Hence, we might use the share of schoolmates living in problem housing estates as an instrument for ethnic concentration in the school. About 20% of the PISA-Ethnic sample live in problem housing estates. The criteria for being a problem housing estate include a number of different elements, many of which are exogenous. However, the main concern with this instrument is that the "problem indicator" partly depends on the share of residents from ethnic minorities. Therefore, we decided that this instrument is not valid, even though there is a strong positive correlation between the share of schoolmates in problem housing estates and the ethnic concentration in the school. We did, however, additionally perform all the estimations with both instruments included at the same time. This only changed the

[18]As an alternative to this instrument, we have also performed all the estimations using ethnic concentration in labor market regions as an instrument. Our labor market regions are commuting areas that are formed such that a large fraction of the residents in a given region work within the region. It is based on data from the Danish Ministry of Environment and Energy, and their grouping of municipalities results in 45 commuting areas. Using this alternative instrument does not change any of the results noticeably, and hence the results are not reported, but they are available from the authors upon request.

	first stage	t-statistics	IV coef.
constant	-1.30	-0.58	381.61**
ethnic concentration	-	-	-0.27
1st gen. immigrant (0/1)	18.02**	15.84	-21.54**
2nd gen. immigrant (0/1)	19.94**	20.20	-9.74
years since migration	0.41**	3.76	-0.39
girl (0/1)	0.42	1.19	26.31**
father's length of edu. (years)	-0.28**	-4.06	2.80**
mother's length of edu. (years)	-0.16**	-2.47	2.69**
family gross income (/DKK 100,000)	-0.25**	-4.27	1.17**
father's occ., self-empl. (0/1)	-2.91**	-4.03	-2.67
father's occ., high level (0/1)	-0.95*	-1.67	14.96**
father's occ., not working (0/1)	0.18	0.28	-0.90
mother's occ., self-empl. (0/1)	-0.32	-0.33	-1.18
mother's occ., high level (0/1)	-1.25**	-2.02	19.99**
mother's occ., not working (0/1)	1.02*	1.80	-7.66**
father's work exp. (years)	-0.06*	-1.84	0.21
mother's work exp. (years)	-0.07*	-1.95	0.01
speak Danish at home (0/1)	-1.46*	-1.68	29.52**
number of siblings	0.60**	4.25	-2.56**
index: cultural possessions (-1.65;1.15)	-0.45**	-2.22	10.80**
more than 500 books (0/1)	0.11	0.18	10.19**
quiet place to study (0/1)	-0.87*	-1.75	13.60**
ethnic conc. in the county	3.48**	45.15	-
obs	7420		7420

**: significant at the 5% level, *: significant at the 10% level.

Table 4: IV estimation results using an instrumental variable to instrument for ethnic concentration. WLE reading score is the dependent variable, pooled sample of PISA-2000 and PISA-Ethnic.

results marginally.[19]

Table 4 shows the estimation results from using the instrumental variable method with ethnic concentration in the county as an instrument for ethnic concentration in the schools. Compared to Model 3 of Table 2 with OLS estimates, we see that the magnitude of the coefficients is very stable. The coefficient of the instrumented variable, ethnic concentration, even increases slightly from the OLS estimates to the IV estimates, although it is no longer significant. According to the IV estimates, a 10%-point increase in ethnic concentration reduces child reading scores by 2.7 points. This may not sound like much, but moving a child from a school with few non-Western immigrants to a school where the ethnic concentration is almost 100% reduces the child's test score by about 27 points. On the other hand, this is about the same magnitude as many of the other effects found, e.g. those of gender, speaking Danish at home, or some of the occupational characteristics of the parents. Hence,

[19]The results are not reported, but they are available from the authors upon request.

ethnic concentration is only one factor among a number of important determinants of children's cognitive outcomes.

The stability of the coefficients between estimation methods points in the direction that we might be better off using OLS estimates, since they by definition have smaller standard errors. Instrumenting for ethnic concentration does not change results much, a fact which is also confirmed by a Hausman test for endogeneity. Results from separate analyses for immigrant children and native Danish children are reported in Tables 11 and 12 in Appendix B. Table 11 shows that the coefficient for ethnic concentration remains significant and negative for the subsample of native Danes even after taking the possible endogeneity into account, whereas it is negative but insignificant for the immigrant subsample as shown in Table 12.

5.2.1 Strength of Instruments

An instrument is strong if the instrumental variable is highly correlated with the endogenous variable, in this case ethnic concentration. The raw correlation between ethnic concentration in the county and ethnic concentration in the school is 0.41, which is a fairly strong positive correlation. The first stage t-statistic is reported in Table 4, where the instrument is included in the estimation. The instrumental variable is positively related to ethnic concentration and it is highly statistically significant. When the first stage t-statistic is high, the instrument is strong. This t-statistic therefore convinces us about the strength of the instrument; see also Staiger and Stock (1997). One of the key identifying assumptions for the instrument is therefore fulfilled. We still need to ensure that the instrument is not only strong, but also valid. Otherwise, the IV estimates may be unreliable.

5.2.2 Validity of Instruments

It is well known that the exclusion restriction cannot be directly verified, that is, we cannot test whether the instrumental variable is uncorrelated with the error term in Equation (3); see e.g. Angrist et al. (1996). We therefore simply argue for the validity of the instrument, more specifically as in Dustmann and Preston (2001), since we also use ethnic concentration in a larger geographical area as an instrument for local ethnic concentration.

It seems reasonable that individuals have no control of the ethnic concentration in a larger geographical area, e.g. a county, and that choice of housing is not based on the general level of ethnic concentration in the county. It is also possible that individuals are geographically limited in their choice of housing by employment and family relations which restrict them to living in a certain geographical area. Further, ethnic concentration in a larger geographical area is very unlikely to affect child outcomes directly. Using the county as the larger geographical area, this would be the case since the counties (a) are large, (b) contain many schools and (c) have schools with different ethnic concentration levels. On the other hand, it is very likely that individuals choose housing *locally* on the basis of unobserved attributes that also affect child outcomes, e.g. the ethnic concentration in the neighborhood, which means that local ethnic concentration is endogenous to child outcome.

Ethnic concentration in larger areas turns out to be highly correlated with ethnic concentration in schools (with the correlation being 0.41), so ethnic concentration in the county seems to be a good instrument for local ethnic concentration. Sorting within the county does not alter the overall ethnic composition of the county and therefore does not alter the validity of the instrument. The main problem with this instrument is that individuals might not be restricted to living in certain geographical areas. If individuals' choice of geographical area is driven by unobserved components, the instrument is not valid. Then we should be concerned that unobserved individual attributes across larger geographical areas might be systematically different.

5.3 School Fixed Effects Estimation

We now take school fixed effects into account in the analysis. This allows us to remove any observable as well as unobservable effects that are fixed within schools. The descriptive statistics in Table 1 suggested possible systematic differences between PISA-Ethnic and PISA-2000 children's schools, and these (fixed) systematic differences are taken into account in the school FE estimation. The effect of ethnic concentration, for example, is taken into account, since ethnic concentration is constant within schools. One can also imagine that a particular school principal may affect child outcomes through his or her goals for the school and the teachers, or that the average teacher quality may differ systematically between schools, e.g. due to teachers' self-selection according to ethnic concentration in the schools. Such potential effects will also be removed in the school fixed effects specification.

Table 5 shows the parameter estimates obtained from the school FE model. Compared to OLS estimates in Model 3 of Table 2, most of the FE estimates are slightly smaller in absolute value. The exceptions are the coefficients to the indicators for having non-Western immigrant background, for both 1st generation and 2nd generation immigrants. The coefficients of the indicators for being a 1st generation or a 2nd generation immigrant of non-Western background are now larger, showing that the test scores are reduced by 32 and 19 points for these individuals respectively. This result may indicate that immigrant children on average attend "better" schools than native Danish children. If children speak Danish with their parents at home, it has a significantly positive effect on their reading score, and the effect is almost identical to that suggested in Table 2. Again, results from separate analyses of immigrant and native Danish children are reported in Appendix B.

6 Conclusion

The school performance of immigrant children is often found to be poor compared to that of native children. In part, this poor performance is caused by inadequate language skills, lower socioeconomic background, and school factors. In this study, we offer evidence on another explanation, namely the effect of going to school with many immigrant peers.

Using a unique and very rich PISA dataset from Denmark, we show that the ethnic concentration in the school influences cognitive outcomes for both immigrant children and native children. Children in schools with a high ethnic concentration score significantly lower on the PISA reading test than children in schools with a low

Explanatory variables	FE-coef.
constant	386.94**
1st gen. immigrant (0/1)	-31.77**
2nd gen. immigrant (0/1)	-18.62**
years since migration	-0.37
girl (0/1)	25.58**
father's length of edu. (years)	2.61**
mother's length of edu. (years)	2.54**
family gross income (/DKK 100,000)	0.91*
father's occ., self-empl. (0/1)	-2.18
father's occ., high level (0/1)	11.50**
father's occ., not working (0/1)	0.46
mother's occ., self-empl. (0/1)	0.52
mother's occ., high level (0/1)	19.50**
mother's occ., not working (0/1)	-6.22*
father's work exp. (years)	0.19
mother's work exp. (years)	-0.09
speak Danish at home (0/1)	28.74**
number of siblings	-2.29**
index: cultural possessions (-1.65;1.15)	9.50**
more than 500 books (0/1)	8.62**
quiet place to study (0/1)	12.17**
R-squared within	0.18
R-squared between	0.41
R-squared overall	0.24
obs	7420

**: significant at the 5% level, *: significant at the 10% level.

Table 5: Estimation results from school fixed effects estimation using WLE reading score as the dependent variable. Pooled sample of PISA-2000 and PISA-Ethnic.

ethnic concentration. Schools with an ethnic concentration above 50% seem to drive this result, especially for native Danish children, but only 3% of the native Danish children in our sample attend schools with an ethnic concentration of more than 50%. For immigrant children, the negative effect of ethnic concentration appears already at a level of 5% ethnic concentration, while the effect is similar in magnitude for all schools with an ethnic concentration above 5%. None of these effects are significant when estimating only on the sample of immigrant children, though. We also find that ethnic background in itself matters, as children from non-Western countries tend to have lower reading test scores than native Danish children. Finally, the results show that speaking Danish at home is strongly correlated with the children's cognitive outcome. This is not surprising given that the children are tested in (Danish) reading abilities.

The negative effects associated with having a non-Western immigrant background and with attending a school with a high ethnic concentration are fairly robust across estimation methods. Taking school fixed effects into account reveals a somewhat stronger association between ethnic background and reading score and further indicates that immigrant children on average attend better schools than native Danish children. Instrumenting for ethnic concentration reveals that after taking into consideration that individuals may sort across neighborhoods, the child's own ethnicity is still important in determining the child's cognitive outcome. Furthermore, ethnic concentration in the school continues to be significantly negatively related to reading scores for native Danish children. Thus, the effect of ethnic concentration in schools on children's reading abilities represents a causal effect and not only a selection effect for the native Danish children.

The negative effect on children's reading scores is not huge, however, with a 10 percentage-point increase in ethnic concentration leading to a reduction in the PISA reading score of about 2.7 points. This must be related to the reading score distribution, which has a mean score of 500 points and a standard deviation of 100. Despite the relatively small effect of ethnic concentration, it is important to remember that a higher fraction of children with immigrant background attend schools with a high ethnic concentration, so they are to a higher degree exposed to the negative effect of ethnic concentration.

The results also show that family background plays an important role in determining child outcomes. Immigrant children have a lower socioeconomic status than native Danes and this is the main reason for immigrant children's lower reading score, according to our results. We can therefore recommend that policy makers do not focus only on ethnic concentration in schools, since ethnic concentration is just one of several determinants of child outcomes and by far not the most important. It seems reasonable, though, to limit ethnic concentration to 50%, since this is the level where the negative effect of ethnic concentration kicks in for native Danish children as well.

Allocating more resources to collecting detailed datasets with test scores for the same children and their siblings over time is important in the future. This type of data will permit panel analyses taking observed and unobserved individual and family fixed effects into account. Further, observing the children from an earlier age provides much more precise indicators of the school factors that are important for child outcomes. The 9th grade outcome is an accumulated result of all the child's experiences both at home and at school, so it is not only the ethnic concentration in

9th grade that matters for the child's final outcome.

Finally, national tests could be a very useful tool both for following children's development and for comparing children across schools and over time. An analysis of national test scores as a basis for these analyses would substantially increase the sample size and provide even more reliable information on both reading and mathematics scores.

References

Allerup, P. (2005). PISA præstationer - målinger med skæve målestokke? *Dansk Pædagogisk Tidsskrift 53*(1), 68–81.

Ammermüller, A. (2007). Poor Background or Low Returns? Why Immigrant Students in Germany Perform so Poorly in PISA. *Education Economics 15*, 215–230.

Ammermüller, A. and J.-S. Pischke (2006). Peer Effects in European Primary Schools: Evidence from PIRLS. *IZA Discussion Paper No. 2077*.

Andersen, A. M., N. Egelund, T. P. Jensen, M. Krone, L. Lindenskov, and J. Mejding (2001). *Forventninger og færdigheder - danske unge i en international sammenligning*. Copenhagen, Denmark: AKF, DPU and SFI-survey.

Angrist, J. D., G. W. Imbens, and D. B. Rubin (1996). Identification of Causal Effects Using Instrumental Variables. *Journal of the American Statistical Association 91*(434), 444–455.

Borjas, G. J. (1995). Ethnicity, Neighborhoods, and Human-Capital Externalities. *American Economic Review 85*(3), 365–390.

Bound, J., D. A. Jaeger, and R. M. Baker (1995). Problems With Instrumental Variables Estimation When the Correlation Between the Instruments and the Endogenous Explanatory Variable is Weak. *Journal of the American Statistical Association 90*(430), 443–450.

Browning, M. and E. Heinesen (2007). Class Size, Teacher Hours and Educational Attainment. *Scandinavian Journal of Economics 109*(2), 415–438.

Damm, A. P. (2009). Determinants of Recent Immigrants' Location Choices: Quasi-Experimental Evidence. *Forthcoming in Journal of Population Economics*.

Dustmann, C. and I. Preston (2001). Attitudes to Ethnic Minorities, Ethnic Context and Location Decisions. *Economic Journal 111*(470), 353–373.

Edin, P.-A., P. Frederiksson, and O. Åslund (2003). Ethnic Enclaves and the Economic Success of Immigrants - Evidence from a Natural Experiment. *Quarterly Journal of Economics 118*(1), 329–357.

Entorf, H. and M. Lauk (2008). Peer Effects, Social Multipliers and Migrants at School: An International Comparison. *Journal of Ethnic and Migration Studies 34*(4), 633–654.

Grönqvist, H. (2006). Ethnic Enclaves and the Attainments of Immigrant Children. *European Sociological Review 22*(4), 369–382.

Hanushek, E. A., J. F. Kain, J. M. Markman, and S. G. Rivkin (2003). Does Peer Ability Affect Student Achievement? *Journal of Applied Econometrics 18*, 527–544.

Hoxby, C. (2000). Peer Effects in the Classroom: Learning from Gender and Race Variation. *NBER Working Paper Series No. 7867.*

Hummelgaard, H., B. K. Graversen, D. Lemmich, and J. B. Nielsen (1997). *Udsatte boligområder i Danmark.* Copenhagen, Denmark: AKF Forlaget.

Jensen, P. and N. Smith (2007). Etnisk koncentration i folkeskolen. In N. Egelund and T. Tranæs (Eds.), *PISA Etnisk 2005*, Chapter 7, pp. 93–130. Rockwool Fondens Forskningsenhed. Syddansk Universitetsforlag.

Manski, C. F. (1993). Identification of Endogenous Social Effects: The Reflection Problem. *Review of Economic Studies 60*(3), 531–542.

OECD (2002). PISA 2000. Technical report, OECD, Paris.

Rangvid, B. S. (2007). Sources of Immigrant's Underachievement: Results from PISA-Copenhagen. *Education Economics 15*, 293–326.

Schnepf, S. V. (2007). Immigrants' Educational Disadvantage: An Examination Across Ten Countries and Three Surveys. *Journal of Population Economics 20*, 527–545.

Staiger, D. and J. H. Stock (1997). Instrumental Variables Regression with Weak Instruments. *Econometrica 65*(3), 557–586.

Szulkin, R. and J. O. Jonsson (2007). Ethnic Segregation and Educational Outcomes in Swedish Comprehensive Schools. *SULCIS Working Papers 2007:2, Stockholm University.*

Todd, P. E. and K. I. Wolpin (2003). On the Specification and Estimation of the Production Function for Cognitive Achievement. *Economic Journal 113*, F3–F33.

Wooldridge, J. M. (2002). *Econometric Analysis of Cross Section and Panel Data.* Cambridge, Massachusetts, London, England: The MIT Press.

A Appendix

Explanatory variables	Model 1	Model 2	Model 3	Model 4
constant	506.22**	368.19**	380.97**	350.65**
ethnic conc. 5-25 (0/1)	-3.42	-6.47*	-4.32	-11.60**
ethnic conc. 25-50 (0/1)	-16.24**	-10.36**	-6.78	-12.13**
ethnic conc. 50-100 (0/1)	-32.27**	-19.88**	-16.92**	-15.87**
1st gen. immigrant (0/1)	-88.62**	-21.01**	-22.87**	-25.82**
2nd gen. immigrant (0/1)	-75.84**	-7.98	-11.71*	-15.32**
years since migration	-0.99	-0.57	-0.41	-0.34
girl (0/1)	25.57**	27.63**	26.29**	25.43**
father's length of edu. (years)		3.32**	2.82**	2.74**
mother's length of edu. (years)		3.33**	2.72**	2.59**
family gross income (/DKK 100,000)		1.50**	1.18**	1.01**
father's occ., self-empl. (0/1)		-0.19	-2.56	-2.43
father's occ., high level (0/1)		20.39**	14.99**	14.48**
father's occ., not working (0/1)		-0.18	-0.82	-0.52
mother's occ., self-empl. (0/1)		1.58	-1.22	0.03
mother's occ., high level (0/1)		26.77**	20.11**	20.37**
mother's occ., not working (0/1)		-6.45*	-7.65**	-7.43**
father's work exp. (years)		0.19	0.22	0.15
mother's work exp. (years)		0.16	0.01	-0.07
speak Danish at home (0/1)		35.58**	29.72**	28.31**
number of siblings		-2.60**	-2.63**	-2.38**
index: cultural possessions (-1.65;1.15)			10.75**	10.33**
more than 500 books (0/1)			10.17**	10.34**
quiet place to study (0/1)			13.71**	13.23**
living in probl. housing estate (0/1)				-8.91*
private school (0/1)				-3.94
number of students				0.05**
teacher/student ratio				30.64
index: time spent on homework (1-4)				7.21**
R-squared	0.13	0.22	0.24	0.25
obs	7420	7420	7420	7420

**: significant at the 5% level, *: significant at the 10% level.

Table 6: OLS estimation results using WLE reading score as the dependent variable and including dummies for ethnic concentration. Pooled sample of PISA-2000 and PISA-Ethnic.

B Appendix

	Pooled sample		PISA-2000		PISA-Ethnic	
	mean	std.dev.	mean	std.dev.	mean	std.dev.
WLE-test score, reading	499.75	98.00	502.21*	96.37	496.25	100.20
ethnic concentration	12.15	15.05	4.63*	8.09	22.88	16.14
ethnic conc. 0-5 (0/1)	0.44	0.50	0.70*	0.46	0.06	0.24
ethnic conc. 5-25 (0/1)	0.40	0.49	0.26*	0.44	0.60	0.49
ethnic conc. 25-50 (0/1)	0.13	0.34	0.04*	0.19	0.27	0.45
ethnic conc. 50-100 (0/1)	0.03	0.17	0.00*	0.03	0.07	0.26
share sch.mates in probl.hous.estate	8.21	15.34	3.61*	8.92	14.76	19.60
eth.conc. in the county	4.98	2.35	3.96*	1.75	6.44	2.34
ethnic conc. in the commuting area	4.63	2.79	3.86*	2.31	5.73	3.02
girl (0/1)	0.50	0.50	0.50	0.50	0.50	0.50
student 16 y.o. (0/1)	0.05	0.21	0.00*	0.00	0.11	0.32
father's length of edu. (years)	12.18	2.83	12.06*	2.79	12.35	2.89
mother's length of edu. (years)	12.11	2.72	11.89*	2.78	12.42	2.59
family gross income (/DKK 100,000)	5.44	4.27	5.36	4.60	5.55	3.73
father's occ., self-empl. (0/1)	0.10	0.30	0.13*	0.33	0.06	0.25
father's occ., high level (0/1)	0.22	0.42	0.22	0.41	0.23	0.42
father's occ., medium/low level (0/1)	0.59	0.49	0.58	0.49	0.60	0.49
father's occ., not working (0/1)	0.09	0.28	0.08*	0.27	0.10	0.30
mother's occ., self-empl. (0/1)	0.04	0.19	0.05*	0.21	0.03	0.17
mother's occ., high level (0/1)	0.15	0.35	0.15	0.35	0.14	0.35
mother's occ., medium/low level (0/1)	0.68	0.47	0.68	0.47	0.68	0.47
mother's occ., not working (0/1)	0.13	0.34	0.13*	0.33	0.15	0.35
father's work exp. (years)	20.08	7.48	19.81*	7.33	20.48	7.67
mother's work exp. (years)	16.03	7.13	15.62*	6.96	16.62	7.32
speak Danish at home (0/1)	0.98	0.14	0.98	0.15	0.98	0.13
number of siblings	1.86	1.28	1.87	1.26	1.85	1.30
index: cultural possessions (-1.65;1.15)	-0.07	0.97	-0.10*	0.97	-0.04	0.97
more than 500 books (0/1)	0.14	0.34	0.13	0.34	0.14	0.35
quiet place to study (0/1)	0.85	0.36	0.87*	0.33	0.81	0.39
living in problem housing estate (0/1)	0.05	0.21	0.02*	0.14	0.08	0.28
private school (0/1)	0.16	0.37	0.23*	0.42	0.04	0.19
number of students	480.24	208.43	422.35*	207.84	583.14	165.39
number of students per class	20.16	2.09	19.94*	2.06	20.45	2.09
teacher/student ratio	0.04	0.07	0.04*	0.06	0.05	0.07
index: time spent on homework (1-4)	2.55	0.59	2.58*	0.60	2.51	0.59
obs	6171		3628		2543	

Note: * indicates that the mean value is significantly different in PISA-2000 and PISA-Ethnic.

Table 7: Means table for Danish children.

	Pooled sample		PISA-2000		PISA-Ethnic	
	mean	std.dev.	mean	std.dev.	mean	std.dev.
WLE-test score, reading	407.24	104.10	417.81	92.92	405.36	105.90
ethnic concentration	43.65	26.54	24.81*	21.88	47.00	25.89
ethnic conc. 0-5 (0/1)	0.02	0.13	0.08*	0.27	0.01	0.09
ethnic conc. 5-25 (0/1)	0.28	0.45	0.52*	0.50	0.23	0.42
ethnic conc. 25-50 (0/1)	0.35	0.48	0.33	0.47	0.35	0.48
ethnic conc. 50-100 (0/1)	0.36	0.48	0.07*	0.25	0.41	0.49
share sch.mates in probl.hous.estate	32.98	28.47	17.81*	18.36	35.69	29.10
eth.conc. in the county	6.89	2.38	5.45*	2.06	7.14	2.35
ethnic conc. in the commuting area	6.04	2.95	5.24*	2.68	6.18	2.98
1st gen. immigrant (0/1)	0.47	0.50	0.67*	0.47	0.43	0.50
2nd gen. immigrant (0/1)	0.53	0.50	0.33*	0.47	0.57	0.50
years since migration	12.62	3.63	11.12*	4.29	12.89	3.43
girl (0/1)	0.53	0.50	0.49	0.50	0.53	0.50
student 16 y.o. (0/1)	0.22	0.42	0.00*	0.00	0.26	0.44
father's length of edu. (years)	9.99	4.31	10.55	3.95	9.90	4.36
mother's length of edu. (years)	8.47	4.83	8.17	5.14	8.52	4.77
family gross income (/DKK 100,000)	2.92	1.51	2.80	1.35	2.94	1.54
father's occ., self-empl. (0/1)	0.11	0.31	0.15*	0.36	0.10	0.30
father's occ., high level (0/1)	0.03	0.16	0.04	0.19	0.02	0.16
father's occ., medium/low level (0/1)	0.36	0.48	0.31	0.46	0.37	0.48
father's occ., not working (0/1)	0.50	0.50	0.50	0.50	0.50	0.50
mother's occ., self-empl. (0/1)	0.03	0.18	0.03	0.16	0.03	0.18
mother's occ., high level (0/1)	0.01	0.11	0.02	0.13	0.01	0.11
mother's occ., medium/low level (0/1)	0.32	0.47	0.32	0.47	0.32	0.47
mother's occ., not working (0/1)	0.64	0.48	0.64	0.48	0.64	0.48
father's work exp. (years)	5.96	6.37	6.20	6.74	5.92	6.31
mother's work exp. (years)	2.49	3.42	2.56	3.78	2.47	3.35
speak Danish at home (0/1)	0.20	0.40	0.24	0.43	0.19	0.40
number of siblings	2.65	1.50	2.54	1.43	2.67	1.51
index: cultural possessions (-1.65;1.15)	-0.66	0.93	-0.57	0.93	-0.68	0.93
more than 500 books (0/1)	0.04	0.20	0.04	0.21	0.04	0.19
quiet place to study (0/1)	0.83	0.38	0.86	0.35	0.82	0.38
living in problem housing estate (0/1)	0.47	0.50	0.36*	0.48	0.49	0.50
private school (0/1)	0.07	0.25	0.18*	0.38	0.05	0.21
number of students	508.58	178.91	463.53*	199.34	517.74	173.19
number of students per class	19.58	2.40	19.65	1.81	19.57	2.48
teacher/student ratio	0.05	0.12	0.10*	0.28	0.04	0.05
index: time spent on homework (1-4)	2.76	0.65	2.83	0.70	2.75	0.64
obs	1249		189		1060	

Note: * indicates that the mean value is significantly different in PISA-2000 and PISA-Ethnic.

Table 8: Means table for immigrant children.

Explanatory variables	Model 1	Model 2	Model 3	Model 4
constant	493.03**	308.98**	331.33**	301.78**
ethnic concentration	-0.55**	-0.34**	-0.28**	-0.37**
girl (0/1)	26.91**	28.72**	27.41**	26.59**
father's length of edu. (years)		3.79**	3.17**	3.06**
mother's length of edu. (years)		5.83**	4.76**	4.65**
family gross income (/DKK 100,000)		1.34**	1.05**	0.91**
father's occ., self-empl. (0/1)		0.91	-0.56	-0.38
father's occ., high level (0/1)		15.41**	11.01**	10.48**
father's occ., not working (0/1)		-0.44	-1.26	-1.24
mother's occ., self-empl. (0/1)		0.41	-3.29	-1.30
mother's occ., high level (0/1)		20.13**	14.70**	15.00**
mother's occ., not working (0/1)		0.82	-0.80	-0.42
father's work exp. (years)		0.09	0.16	0.07
mother's work exp. (years)		0.22	0.08	0.00
speak Danish at home (0/1)		48.99**	44.05**	44.71**
number of siblings		-1.20	-1.57*	-1.21
index: cultural possessions (-1.65;1.15)			11.30**	10.76**
more than 500 books (0/1)			7.82**	8.19**
quiet place to study (0/1)			12.89**	12.52**
living in probl. housing estate (0/1)				-4.17
private school (0/1)				-5.07
number of students				0.04**
teacher/student ratio				22.39
index: time spent on homework (1-4)				7.27**
R-squared	0.03	0.14	0.17	0.18
obs	6171	6171	6171	6171

**: significant at the 5% level, *: significant at the 10% level.

Table 9: OLS estimates for Danish children. Pooled sample of PISA-2000 and PISA-Ethnic.

Explanatory variables	Model 1	Model 2	Model 3	Model 4
constant	395.58**	381.16**	379.53**	340.75**
ethnic concentration	-0.33**	-0.17	-0.18	-0.08
2nd gen. immigrant (0/1)	1.45	-4.30	-3.93	-5.94
years since migration	1.19	1.48	1.47	1.78
girl (0/1)	19.15**	20.63**	20.45**	19.15**
father's length of edu. (years)		2.35**	2.23**	2.26**
mother's length of edu. (years)		0.34	0.27	0.11
family gross income (/DKK 100,000)		2.87	2.68	2.18
father's occ., self-empl. (0/1)		-7.90	-12.45	-13.73
father's occ., high level (0/1)		63.20**	54.74**	49.24**
father's occ., not working (0/1)		6.33	4.31	4.55
mother's occ., self-empl. (0/1)		10.20	8.52	7.63
mother's occ., high level (0/1)		48.85*	42.25	33.72
mother's occ., not working (0/1)		-21.35**	-22.24**	-24.34**
father's work exp. (years)		0.84	0.73	0.63
mother's work exp. (years)		-0.42	-0.73	-0.94
speak Danish at home (0/1)		16.97	16.16	14.00
number of siblings		-7.70	-6.90**	-6.38**
index: cultural possessions (-1.65;1.15)			4.32	3.84
more than 500 books (0/1)			15.62	11.95
quiet place to study (0/1)			14.78*	13.06
living in probl. housing estate (0/1)				-11.65*
private school (0/1)				3.52
number of students				0.03
teacher/student ratio				21.98
index: time spent on homework (1-4)				10.92**
R-squared	0.02	0.10	0.12	0.14
obs	1249	1249	1249	1249

**: significant at the 5% level, *: significant at the 10% level.

Table 10: OLS estimates for immigrant children. Pooled sample of PISA-2000 and PISA-Ethnic.

	first stage	t-statistics	IV coef.
constant	1.60	0.89	331.90**
ethnic concentration	-	-	-0.31*
girl (0/1)	0.28	0.87	27.41**
father's length of edu. (years)	-0.25**	-3.40	3.17**
mother's length of edu. (years)	-0.02	-0.24	4.77**
family gross income (/DKK 100,000)	-0.24**	-4.94	1.05**
father's occ., self-empl. (0/1)	-2.91**	-4.34	-0.74
father's occ., high level (0/1)	-1.19**	-2.42	10.98**
father's occ., not working (0/1)	1.30*	1.92	-1.18
mother's occ., self-empl. (0/1)	-1.11	-1.25	-3.34
mother's occ., high level (0/1)	-1.20**	-2.26	14.65**
mother's occ., not working (0/1)	1.24**	2.25	-0.71
father's work exp. (years)	0.01	0.19	0.16
mother's work exp. (years)	-0.06**	-2.08	0.08
speak Danish at home (0/1)	-0.72	-0.61	43.97**
number of siblings	0.32**	2.42	-1.56
index: cultural possessions (-1.65;1.15)	-0.59**	-3.17	11.30**
more than 500 books (0/1)	-0.08	-0.16	7.82**
quiet place to study (0/1)	-0.88*	-1.93	12.79**
ethnic conc. in the county	3.34**	47.63	-
obs	6171		6171

**: significant at the 5% level, *: significant at the 10% level.

Table 11: IV estimates for Danish children. Pooled sample of PISA-2000 and PISA-Ethnic.

	first stage	t-statistics	IV coef.
constant	16.55**	3.15	385.48**
ethnic concentration	-	-	-0.35
2nd gen. immigrant (0/1)	1.76	0.87	-3.13
years since migration	0.70**	2.72	1.64
girl (0/1)	0.59	0.42	20.71**
father's length of edu. (years)	-0.29	-1.61	2.19**
mother's length of edu. (years)	-0.27*	-1.76	0.22
family gross income (/DKK 100,000)	-0.14	-0.24	2.64
father's occ., self-empl. (0/1)	-2.51	-0.94	-12.23
father's occ., high level (0/1)	-1.24	-0.26	54.64**
father's occ., not working (0/1)	-3.36*	-1.76	3.80
mother's occ., self-empl. (0/1)	2.51	0.60	8.80
mother's occ., high level (0/1)	-17.07**	-2.65	39.45
mother's occ., not working (0/1)	-1.71	-0.89	-22.44**
father's work exp. (years)	-0.31**	-2.08	0.73
mother's work exp. (years)	-0.86**	-2.99	-0.88
speak Danish at home (0/1)	-0.23	-0.12	16.01*
number of siblings	1.44**	2.89	-6.69**
index: cultural possessions (-1.65;1.15)	0.14	0.18	4.26
more than 500 books (0/1)	4.16	1.06	16.96
quiet place to study (0/1)	-1.48	-0.79	14.44*
ethnic conc. in the county	3.97**	12.78	-
obs	1249		1249

**: significant at the 5% level, *: significant at the 10% level.

Table 12: IV estimates for immigrant children. Pooled sample of PISA-2000 and PISA-Ethnic.

Explanatory variables	FE-coef.
constant	340.78**
girl (0/1)	26.87**
father's length of edu. (years)	2.94**
mother's length of edu. (years)	4.42**
family gross income (/DKK 100,000)	0.78*
father's occ., self-empl. (0/1)	0.56
father's occ., high level (0/1)	8.88**
father's occ., not working (0/1)	2.46
mother's occ., self-empl. (0/1)	-1.44
mother's occ., high level (0/1)	14.98**
mother's occ., not working (0/1)	1.37
father's work exp. (years)	0.12
mother's work exp. (years)	-0.04
speak Danish at home (0/1)	42.82**
number of siblings	-1.05
index: cultural possessions (-1.65;1.15)	9.86**
more than 500 books (0/1)	7.22*
quiet place to study (0/1)	10.97**
R-squared within	0.13
R-squared between	0.43
R-squared overall	0.17
obs	6171

**: significant at the 5% level, *: significant at the 10% level.

Table 13: School FE estimates for Danish children. Pooled sample of PISA-2000 and PISA-Ethnic.

Explanatory variables	FE-coef.
constant	381.65**
2nd gen. immigrant (0/1)	-1.16
years since migration	1.17
girl (0/1)	18.14**
mother's length of edu. (years)	2.20**
family gross income (/DKK 100,000)	0.03
father's length of edu. (years)	2.18
father's occ., self-empl. (0/1)	-15.56
father's occ., high level (0/1)	54.88**
father's occ., not working (0/1)	5.72
mother's occ., self-empl. (0/1)	-2.08
mother's occ., high level (0/1)	31.92
mother's occ., not working (0/1)	-27.11**
father's work exp. (years)	1.00
mother's work exp. (years)	-0.93
speak Danish at home (0/1)	13.31
number of siblings	-5.26**
index: cultural possessions (-1.65;1.15)	4.67
more than 500 books (0/1)	19.62
quiet place to study (0/1)	11.61
R-squared within	0.12
R-squared between	0.07
R-squared overall	0.11
obs	6171

**: significant at the 5% level, *: significant at the 10% level.

Table 14: School FE estimates for immigrant children. Pooled sample of PISA-2000 and PISA-Ethnic.

Explanatory variables	Model 1	Model 2	Model 3	Model 4
constant	490.81**	308.65**	331.06**	300.58**
ethnic conc. 5-25 (0/1)	-2.26	-6.57*	-4.53	-11.85**
ethnic conc. 25-50 (0/1)	-16.60**	-9.74**	-6.94	-13.81**
ethnic conc. 50-100 (0/1)	-44.83**	-27.37**	-23.73**	-23.53**
girl (0/1)	26.86**	28.69**	27.40**	26.59**
father's length of edu. (years)		3.83**	3.19**	3.08**
mother's length of edu. (years)		5.83**	4.75**	4.69**
family gross income (/DKK 100,000)		1.35**	1.05**	0.90*
father's occ., self-empl. (0/1)		1.02	-0.49	-0.46
father's occ., high level (0/1)		15.43**	11.05**	10.58**
father's occ., not working (0/1)		-0.32	-1.24	-1.06
mother's occ., self-empl. (0/1)		0.19	-3.36	-1.57
mother's occ., high level (0/1)		20.24**	14.81**	15.19**
mother's occ., not working (0/1)		0.87	-0.76	-0.10
father's work exp. (years)		0.12	0.16	0.08
mother's work exp. (years)		0.22	0.08	0.01
speak Danish at home (0/1)		49.21**	44.37**	44.95**
number of siblings		-1.28	-1.61	-1.32
index: cultural possessions (-1.65;1.15)			11.26**	10.79**
more than 500 books (0/1)			7.90**	8.24**
quiet place to study (0/1)			12.91**	12.37**
living in probl. housing estate (0/1)				-5.46
private school (0/1)				-5.65
number of students				0.05**
teacher/student ratio				28.19
index: time spent on homework (1-4)				7.22**
R-squared	0.03	0.14	0.17	0.18
obs	6171	6171	6171	6171

**: significant at the 5% level, *: significant at the 10% level.

Table 15: OLS estimates for Danish children with dummies for ethnic concentration included. Pooled sample of PISA-2000 and PISA-Ethnic.

Explanatory variables	Model 1	Model 2	Model 3	Model 4
constant	414.71**	400.71**	394.44**	358.89**
ethnic conc. 5-25 (0/1)	-26.36	-25.58	-21.15	-25.75
ethnic conc. 25-50 (0/1)	-31.02	-28.36	-22.83	-21.31
ethnic conc. 50-100 (0/1)	-42.52*	-32.29	-27.79	-24.19
2nd gen. immigrant (0/1)	0.89	-5.10	-4.44	-6.63
years since migration	1.20	1.53	1.48	1.77
girl (0/1)	19.31**	20.84**	20.74**	19.57**
father's length of edu. (years)		2.36**	2.24**	2.25**
mother's length of edu. (years)		0.36	0.29	0.12
family gross income (/DKK 100,000)		2.96	2.77	2.19
father's occ., self-empl. (0/1)		-8.05	-12.64	-13.64
father's occ., high level (0/1)		64.21**	55.32**	49.76**
father's occ., not working (0/1)		6.58	4.66	4.88
mother's occ., self-empl. (0/1)		10.81	8.91	7.83
mother's occ., high level (0/1)		50.42*	44.03	35.34
mother's occ., not working (0/1)		-21.15**	-22.09**	-24.32**
father's work exp. (years)		0.82	0.73	0.61
mother's work exp. (years)		-0.29	-0.66	-0.87
speak Danish at home (0/1)		16.85*	16.04*	13.73
number of siblings		-7.70**	-6.99**	-6.40**
index: cultural possessions (-1.65;1.15)			4.14	3.85
more than 500 books (0/1)			13.93	9.36
quiet place to study (0/1)			14.99*	13.39
living in probl. housing estate (0/1)				-12.85*
private school (0/1)				2.45
number of students				0.03
teacher/student ratio				23.71
index: time spent on homework (1-4)				10.68**
R-squared	0.01	0.10	0.12	0.14
obs	1249	1249	1249	1249

**: significant at the 5% level, *: significant at the 10% level.

Table 16: OLS estimates for immigrant children with dummies for ethnic concentration included. Pooled sample of PISA-2000 and PISA-Ethnic.

Publications in English from the Rockwool Foundation Research Unit

Time and Consumption
Edited by Gunnar Viby Mogensen. With contributions by Søren Brodersen, Thomas Gelting, Niels Buus Kristensen, Eszter Körmendi, Lisbeth Pedersen, Benedicte Madsen. Niels Ploug, Erik Ib Schmidt, Rewal Schmidt Sørensen, and Gunnar Viby Mogensen (Statistics Denmark, Copenhagen. 1990)

Danes and Their Politicians
By Gunnar Viby Mogensen (Aarhus University Press. 1993)

Solidarity or Egoism?
By Douglas A. Hibbs (Aarhus University Press. 1993)

Welfare and Work Incentives. A North European Perspective
Edited by A.B. Atkinson and Gunnar Viby Mogensen. With Contributions by A.B. Atkinson, Richard Blundell, Björn Gustafsson, Anders Klevmarken, Peder J. Pedersen, and Klaus Zimmermann (Oxford University Press. 1993)

Unemployment and Flexibility on the Danish Labour Market
By Gunnar Viby Mogensen (Statistics Denmark, Copenhagen. 1994)

On the Measurement of a Welfare Indicator for Denmark 1970-1990
By Peter Rørmose Jensen and Elisabeth Møllgaard (Statistics Denmark, Copenhagen. 1995)

The Shadow Economy in Denmark 1994. Measurement and Results
By Gunnar Viby Mogensen, Hans Kurt Kvist, Eszter Körmendi, and Søren Pedersen (Statistics Denmark, Copenhagen. 1995)

Work Incentives in the Danish Welfare State: New Empirical Evidence
Edited by Gunnar Viby Mogensen. With contributions by Søren Brodersen, Lisbeth Pedersen, Peder J. Pedersen, Søren Pedersen, and Nina Smith (Aarhus University Press. 1995)

Actual and Potential Recipients of Welfare Benefits with a Focus on Housing Benefits, 1987-1992
By Hans Hansen and Marie Louise Hultin (Statistics Denmark, Copenhagen. 1997)

The Shadow Economy in Western Europe. Measurement and Results for Selected Countries
By Søren Pedersen. With contributions by Esben Dalgaard and Gunnar Viby Mogensen (Statistics Denmark, Copenhagen. 1998)

Immigration to Denmark. International and National Perspectives
By David Coleman and Eskil Wadensjö. With contributions by Bent Jensen and Søren Pedersen (Aarhus University Press. 1999)

Nature as a Political Issue in the Classical Industrial Society: The Environmental Debate in the Danish Press from the 1870s to the 1970s
By Bent Jensen (Statistics Denmark, Copenhagen. 2000)

Foreigners in the Danish newspaper debate from the 1870s to the 1990s
By Bent Jensen (Statistics Denmark, Copenhagen. 2001)

The integration of non-Western immigrants in a Scandinavian labour market: The Danish experience
By Marie Louise Schultz-Nielsen. With contributions by Olaf Ingerslev, Claus Larsen, Gunnar Viby Mogensen, Niels-Kenneth Nielsen, Søren Pedersen, and Eskil Wadensjö (Statistics Denmark, Copenhagen. 2001)

Immigration and the public sector in Denmark
By Eskil Wadensjö and Helena Orrje (Aarhus University Press. 2002)

Social security in Denmark and Germany – with a focus on access conditions for refugees and immigrants. A comparative study
By Hans Hansen, Helle Cwarzko Jensen, Claus Larsen, and Niels-Kenneth Nielsen (Statistics Denmark, Copenhagen. 2002)

The Shadow Economy in Germany, Great Britain, and Scandinavia. A measurement based on questionnaire surveys
By Søren Pedersen (Statistics Denmark, Copenhagen. 2003)

Do-it-yourself work in North-Western Europe. Maintenance and improvement of homes
By Søren Brodersen (Statistics Denmark, Copenhagen. 2003)

Migrants, Work, and the Welfare State
Edited by Torben Tranæs and Klaus F. Zimmermann. With contributions by Thomas Bauer, Amelie Constant, Horst Entorf, Christer Gerdes, Claus Larsen, Poul Chr. Matthiessen, Niels-Kenneth Nielsen, Marie Louise Schultz-Nielsen, and Eskil Wadensjö (University Press of Southern Denmark. 2004)

Black Activities in Germany in 2001 and in 2004. A Comparison Based on Survey Data
By Lars P. Feld and Claus Larsen (Statistics Denmark, Copenhagen. 2005)

From Asylum Seeker to Refugee to Family Reunification. Welfare Payments in These Situations in Various Western Countries
By Hans Hansen (Statistics Denmark, Copenhagen. 2006)

A Comparison of Welfare Payments to Asylum Seekers, Refugees, and Reunified Families. In Selected European Countries and in Canada
By Torben Tranæs, Bent Jensen, and Mark Gervasini Nielsen (Statistics Denmark, Copenhagen. 2006)

Employment Effects of Reducing Welfare to Refugees
By Duy T. Huynh, Marie Louise Schultz-Nielsen and Torben Tranæs (The Rockwool Foundation Research Unit. 2007)

Determination of Net Transfers for Immigrants in Germany
By Christer Gerdes (The Rockwool Foundation Research Unit. 2007)

What happens to the Employment of Native Co-Workers when Immigrants are Hired?
By Nikolaj Malchow-Møller, Jakob Roland Munch, and Jan Rose Skaksen (The Rockwool Foundation Research Unit. 2007)

Immigrants at the Workplace and the Wages of Native Workers
By Nikolaj Malchow-Møller, Jakob Roland Munch, and Jan Rose Skaksen (The Rockwool Foundation Research Unit. 2007)

Crime and Partnerships
By Michael Svarer (University Press of Southern Denmark, The Rockwool Foundation Research Unit. 2008)

The Unemployed in the Danish Newspaper Debate from the 1840s to the 1990s
By Bent Jensen (University Press of Southern Denmark, The Rockwool Foundation Research Unit. 2008)

Immigrant and Native Children's Cognitive Outcomes and the Effect of Ethnic Concentration in Danish Schools
By Peter Jensen and Astrid Würtz Rasmussen (University Press of Southern Denmark, The Rockwool Foundation Research Unit. 2008)

The Rockwool Foundation Research Unit on the Internet

Completely updated information, e.g. about the latest projects of the Research Unit, can always be found on the Internet under the home page of the Research Unit at the address: www.rff.dk

The home page includes in a Danish and an English version:

- a commented survey of publications stating distributors of the books of the Reseach Unit
- survey of research projects
- information about the organization and staff of the Research Unit
- information about data base and choice of method and
- newsletters from the Research Unit

Printed newsletters free of charge from the Rockwool Foundation Research Unit can also be ordered on telephone +45 39 17 38 32.